ONE MO' TIME. [Libretto]

An Evening at the Lyric Theatre 1926

Concept and Book by

Vernel Bagneris

No part of this book may be reproduced, stored in a retrieval system, or transmitted in any form, by any means, including mechanical, electronic, photocopying, recording, or otherwise, without the prior written permission of the publisher.

SAMUEL FRENCH, INC.
45 WEST 25TH STREET   NEW YORK 10010
7623 SUNSET BOULEVARD   HOLLYWOOD 90046
LONDON   TORONTO

782.812
BAGNERIS

Book Copyright © 1979 by Vernel Bagneris
ALL RIGHTS RESERVED

Amateurs wishing to arrange for the production of ONE MO' TIME must make application to SAMUEL FRENCH, INC., at 45 West 25th Street, New York N.Y. 10010, giving the following particulars:

(1) The name of the town and theatre or hall in which it is proposed to give the production.
(2) The maximum seating capacity of the theatre or hall.
(3) Scale of ticket prices.
(4) The number of performances it is intended to give, and the dates thereof.
(5) Indicate whether you will use an orchestration or simply a piano.

Upon receipt of these particulars SAMUEL FRENCH, INC., will quote terms and availability.

Stock royalty quoted on application to SAMUEL FRENCH, INC., 45 West 25th Street, New York, N.Y. 10010.

For all other rights than those stipulated above apply to Michael Lee Hertzberg, Esq., 275 Madison Ave., New York, N.Y. 10016.

An orchestration consisting of:

Piano/conductor's score
Clarinet
Tuba
Trumpet
Drums

will be loaned two months prior to the production ONLY on receipt of the royalty quoted for all performances, the rental fee and a refundable deposit. The deposit will be refunded on the safe return to SAMUEL FRENCH, INC. of all materials loaned for the production.

Anyone presenting the play shall not commit or authorize any act or omission by which the copyright of the play or the right to copyright same may be impaired.

No changes shall be made in the play for the purpose of your production unless authorized in writing.

The publication of this play does not imply that it is necessarily available for performance by amateurs or professionals. Amateurs and professionals considering a production are strongly advised in their own interests to apply to Samuel French, Inc., for consent before starting rehearsals, advertising, or booking a theatre or hall.

Printed in U.S.A.
ISBN 0 573 68159 7

"After You've Gone" by Henry Creamer and J. Rurner Layton. Copyright ©, 1918, 1946, by Morley Music Co.
"My Man Blues" by Bessie Smith. Copyright ©, 1926, 1954, 1974, by Frank Music Corp.
"Hindustan" by Oliver G. Wallace and H. Weeks. Copyright ©, 1918, by Melody Shop. Copyright ©, 1946 by Harold Weeks. Assigned in 1946 to Fred Fischer Music Co., Inc. Assigned in 1953 to Venus Music Corp.
"New Orleans Hop Scop Blues" by George W. Thomas. Copyright ©, 1923, by Charles Williams Music Publishing Co., Inc. Copyright ©, 1951, by Jerry Vogel Music Co., Inc.
"A Hot Time in the Old Town": Public Domain.
"Down in Honky Tonk Town" by Charles McCarron & C. Smith. Copyright ©, 1916, by Broadway Music (ASCAP). Copyright ©, 1943, by Le-Mor. Present publishers: Christie-Max Music & American Broadcast Music, Inc.
"Black Bottom" by Ray Henderson, BG de Sylva & Lew Brown. Copyright ©, 1926, 1953, by Warner Bros., Inc.
"She's Funny That Way" by Richard Whiting & Neil Moret. Copyright, ©, 1928, 1928, by Chappell Music Co., Inc. Copyright Renewed.
"Muddy Waters" by Jo Trent, Peter De Rose & Harry Richman. Copyright ©, 1926, 1953 by Broadway Music Corp.
"Muskrat Ramble" by Edward "Kid" Ohry. Copyright ©, 1926 by Janeiro Music Co. Assigned to George Simon, Inc. Copyright renewed.
"EVERYBODY LOVES MY BABY
(But My Baby Don't Love Nobody But Me)"
Words and Music by JACK PALMER and SPENCER WILLIAMS
© Copyright 1924 by MCA MUSIC PUBLISHING, A Division of MCA INC., New York, NY 10019. Copyright renewed.
USED BY PERMISSION   ALL RIGHTS RESERVED
"KITCHEN MAN"
By ANDY RAZAF and ALEX BELLENDA
© Copyright 1929 by MCA MUSIC PUBLISHING, A Division of MCA INC., New York, NY 10019. Copyright renewed.
USED BY PERMISSION   ALL RIGHTS RESERVED
"SEE SEE RIDER"
Words and Music by MA RAINEY
© Copyright 1943, 1944 by MCA MUSIC PUBLISHING, A Division of MCA INC., New York, NY 10019.
USED BY PERMISSION   ALL RIGHTS RESERVED
"DON'T TURN YOUR BACK ON ME"
By ANDY RAZAF and CLARENCE WILLIAMS
© Copyright 1935 by MCA MUSIC PUBLISHING, A Division of MCA INC., New York, 10019. Copyright renewed.
USED BY PERMISSION   ALL RIGHTS RESERVED
"I'VE GOT WHAT IT TAKES, BUT IT BREAKS MY HEART TO GIVE IT AWAY"
By HEZEKIAH JENKINS and CLARENCE WILLIAMS
© Copyright 1929 by MCA MUSIC PUBLISHING, A Division of MCA INC., New York, NY 10019. Copyright renewed.
USED BY PERMISSION   ALL RIGHTS RESERVED

"PAPA DE DA DA"
By SPENCER WILLIAMS, CLARENCE WILLIAMS and CLARENCE TODD
© Copyright 1925 by MCA MUSIC PUBLISHING, A Division of MCA INC., New York, NY 10019. Copyright renewed.
USED BY PERMISSION   ALL RIGHTS RESERVED

"WAIT TILL YOU SEE MY BABY DO THE CHARLESTON"
By CLARENCE TODD, ROUSSEAU SIMMONS and CLARENCE WILLIAMS
© Copyright 1925 by MCA MUSIC PUBLISHING, A Division of MCA INC., New York, NY 10019. Copyright renewed.
USED BY PERMISSION   ALL RIGHTS RESERVED

"CAKE WALKIN' BABIES FROM HOME"
By CHRIS SMITH, HENRY TROY and CLARENCE WILLIAMS
© Copyright 1925 by MCA MUSIC PUBLISHING, A Division of MCA INC., New York, NY 10019. Copyright renewed.
USED BY PERMISSION   ALL RIGHTS RESERVED

"THE RIGHT KEY BUT THE WRONG KEY HOLE"
By CLARENCE WILLIAMS and EDDIE GREEN
© Copyright 1935 by MCA MUSIC PUBLISHING, A Division of MCA INC., New York, NY 10019. Copyright renewed.
USED BY PERMISSION   ALL RIGHTS RESERVED

All licenses granted by Samuel French, Inc. for stock and amateur performances shall require producers to give credit to Vernel Bagneris as author in all programs, advertising, publicizing or otherwise exploiting the Work. In all instances in which the title of the play appears for advertising, publicizing or exploiting the Work and/or production, the name of the Author must appear on a separate line, in which no other name appears, in a size of type not less than 50% the size of type of the title or stars, whichever is the larger. No other name shall precede the title except the name of any star (there shall be no more than two) and the name of the producer of stock or amateur production.

Billing shall appear in the following form:

(Name of Producer)
presents

ONE MO' TIME
An Evening at the Lyric Theatre 1926

Concept and Book and Original Direction
by

Vernel Bagneris

ONE MO' TIME opened October 22, 1979 at the Village Gate Downstairs. The production was conceived by Vernel Bagneris. Produced by Art D'Lugoff, Burt D'Lugoff and Jerry Wexler in association with Shari Upbin with the following cast:

BERTHA .... Sylvia "Kuumba" Williams
MA REED .... Thais Clark
THELMA .... Topsy Chapman
PAPA DU .... Vernel Bagneris
THEATRE OWNER .... John Stell

New Orleans Blue Serenaders: Lars Edegran piano, co-director; John Robichaux drums; Walter Payton tuba; Jabbo Smith trumpet.

Understudies: Miss Clark-Carol Woods; Mr. Bagneris-Bruce Strickland; Miss Williams-Denise Rogers; Miss Chapman-Peggy Alston; Mr. Stell-James Wilcher.

Directed by Vernel Bagneris; scenery, Elwin Charles Terrel II; costumes, Joann Clevenger; lighting, Joanna Shielke; General Manager, Albert Poland; musical arrangements, Lars Edegran, Orange Kellin; additional staging Dean Irby; sound, Seltzer; production consultant, Pepsi Bethel; production stage manager, Shari Upbin; press, Milly Schoenbaum, Anne Obert Weinberg.

The show was previously produced in New Orleans.

ONE MO' TIME

ACT ONE

[MUSIC #1: *OVERTURE: DARKTOWN STRUTTERS BALL*]

    THEATRE OWNER. (*enters* U.S.C. *hitting piano lid*)
KEEP IT UP!
(*crossing* D.S., *addressing audience*)
ALRIGHT, ALRIGHT, SHUT UP AND SIT DOWN.
SHOW'S ABOUT READY TO START
AND JUST CAUSE YOU PAID YOUR TWENTY-FIVE
  CENTS
TO GIT IN HERE THAT DON'T GIVE YOU THE RIGHT
TO MESS THE PLACE UP.
NOW I DON'T WANT NO SMOKIN, NO DRINKIN
AND I SURE AS HELL DON'T WANT TO FIND NO
FOOT PRINTS ON THAT SEAT IN FRONT OF YOU.
  YA HEAR?
ALRIGHT.
NOW TONIGHT THE LYRIC THEATRE PROUDLY
  PRESENTS
BIG BERTHA WILLIAMS AND HER TOURING
  COMPANY
PROVIN' ONCE AGAIN THAT WE PROVIDE THE BEST
IN COLORED ENTERTAINMENT.
SO LET'S GIT ON WITH THE SHOW
AND Y'ALL HAVE A REAL GOOD TIME
(*starts to leave, stops and turns back*)
AND NO SPITTIN' ON THE FLOOR.
(*to the band on exit* U.S.C.)

[MUSIC #2: *HONKY TONK TOWN*]

    PAPA DU. (*entering* U.S.C. *on intro vamp*)
BILL JOHNSON SAID ONE DAY
TO HIS ELIZA MAE
WE'VE BEEN TO NEARLY EVERY PLACE IN TOWN

IF SUGGEST TO ME
(*MA REED* enters US.R.)
SOME OTHER NOVELTY
WE BOTH WILL GO AND DO THE THING UP BROWN
HIS SWEETIE SAID "MY DEAR, THERE IS A PLACE
  I HEAR
I GOT IT STRAIGHT FROM MOSE
WHO BRINGS THE CLOTHES
IT'S HONKY TONKY TOWN
DOWN WHERE THE GALS ARE BROWN
THAT'S WHERE THAT MUSIC FLOWS"
  CHORUS. (*ALL sing, see sheet music.*)
COME HONEY LET'S GO DOWN,
TO HONKY TONKY TOWN,
IT'S UNDERNEATH THE GROUND,
WHERE ALL THE FUN IS FOUND.
THERE'LL BE SINGING WAITERS,
SINGING SYNCOPATERS
DANCING TO PIANO PLAYED BY MISTER BROWN.
PIANO HE PLAYS MY DEAR,
HE PLAYS IT ALL BY EAR,
YOU'LL WANT TO STAY A YEAR,
THAT MUSIC THAT YOU HEAR.
MAKE YOU ACT A MONKEY,
DANCING TILL YOU'RE FUNKY,
DOWN IN HONKY TONK TOWN.

THAT HULA HULA DANCE,
DON'T EVEN STAND A CHANCE,
YOU GOT TO SEE THEM FOLKS GET DOWN AND
  MEAN.
THEY DO THE TEH-NAH-NAH,
AND THEN YOU KNOW SOMEHOW
YOU MUST BE BACK IN OLD NEW ORLEANS.
IT'S GOT TO BE A FAD,
WITH EVERY GAL AND LAD,
TO GO TO HONKY TONKY TOWN AT NIGHT.
EACH GIRLIE CRIES TO,
AND WHEN SHE SPIES HER BEAU,
SHE YELLS OUT WITH ALL HER MIGHT:
(*repeat chorus*)
COME HONEY LET'S GO DOWN,

TO HONKY TONKY TOWN,
IT'S UNDERNEATH THE GROUND,
WHERE ALL THE FUN IS FOUND.
THERE'LL BE SINGING WAITERS,
SINGING SYNCOPATERS
DANCING TO PIANO PLAYED BY MISTER BROWN.
PIANO HE PLAYS MY DEAR,
HE PLAYS IT ALL BY EAR,
YOU'LL WANT TO STAY A YEAR,
THAT MUSIC THAT YOU HEAR.
MAKE YOU ACT A MONKEY,
DANCING TILL YOU'RE FUNKY,
DOWN IN HONKY TONK TOWN.

(*At the end of HONKY TONK all exit* US.C.)

Scene 1

(*The dressing room. PAPA DU enters first, followed by THELMA and then MA REED who exits into back room.*)

PAPA DU. Now look at this. Agie and Edna ain't here, and God only knows where Bertha's at. Well look, as company manager I'm tellin y'all the show's gonna sit till Bertha git herself in here. (*He sits in his chair. MA exits back dressing area.*)

THELMA. (*seated in her chair*) Well, I know if I was supposed to be the company manager, I wouldn't sit around waitin' on no Bertha.

PAPA DU. You wouldn't, huh?

THELMA. Man, you could ruin your reputation. Nah I can sing that song, an you know it. (*arm on his shoulder*)

PAPA DU. You could, but you ain't. (*THELMA pushes him.*) That's Bertha's song and she don't want nobody copyin' her material.

THELMA. And who needs to copy her material. This is Thelma Marie Scott you talkin to honey. I have my own style thank you. (*standing up behind her chair*) Her material. First, I'd have to blow the dust off her material. Anyway you said last night if she was late again (*MA REED enters and sits in her chair.*) that I could try that number. Remember?

PAPA DU. (*glancing at MA REED*) Maybe we could talk about that some other time.
THELMA. NO.
MA REED. No. Let her be smart. Go on and do it baby. Big Bertha's gonna love for you to do that number. Why she'd whip yo' tail all the way back to the hotel.
THELMA. Well let's just see (*picks up fan from BERTHA's dressing table*) how much tail she can whip tonight. (*She exits to the stage.*)
PAPA DU. (*crossing to door after her*) Now Thelma put that fan down and . . .
MA REED. (*seated, catching him around the waist*) Wait a minute honey. Let the fool go. Now. Speakin of hotels, we got one don't we?
PAPA DU. (*taking down suitcase and putting it on BERTHA's chair, opens it*) Well, not exactly.
MA REED. Not exactly?
PAPA DU. Now look here Ma. I asked the man at the desk about the rates. He said it was five dollars for the first floor, four dollars for the second floor, and three dollars for the third floor. I was turnin to leave, he said "What's the matter aren't our rates alright?" I said "Your rates is fine your hotel just ain't high enough."
MA REED. Well how come we always got to stay in places where hot an cold water means hot in the summer and cold in the winter? (*laughs*)
PAPA DU. Now ma, if you'd just quit all this singin' and dancin' routine an go git yourself married.
MA REED. Married? Oh no honey, not me.
PAPA DU. And why not? (*PAPA DU closes suitcase and puts it back on the shelf.*)
MA REED. Cause nobody don't want to marry me when I'm drunk an I sure as hell don't want to marry nobody when I'm sober. (*laughs*)

[MUSIC #3: *KISS ME SWEET*]

(*PAPA DU and THELMA*)

THELMA. (*entering* US.R. *with small stool, crosses* C.S. *and sits in front of pole, fanning herself*)
I WAS SO BLUE, AND LONELY TOO
YOU WENT AWAY, I WISHED YOU'D STAY

ONE MO' TIME

TO HOLD ME DEAR AND PRESS YOUR LOVING
LIPS TO MINE
   PAPA DU. (*Papa Du entering* US.R. *crosses down stage to* DS.R.)
I THOUGHT I'D DIE, I DON'T KNOW WHY
BUT SEEMS TO ME A CERTAINTY
THAT WAITIN' FOR YOU MAMA WAS NOT A
WASTE OF TIME.
   THELMA. (*Crossing* D.S., *she sings. See sheet music.*) KISS ME
SWEET
   PAPA DU.
I NEED SOME INSPIRATION
   THELMA.
KISS ME SWEET
   PAPA DU.
THRILL ME WITH SENSATION
   THELMA.
HONEY WHEN YOU PRESS YOUR LOVING LIPS TO
MINE
   PAPA DU.
I GET A FUNNY FEELING CREEPING DOWN MY SPINE
   THELMA.
KISS ME NOW
   PAPA DU.
I CAN'T WAIT NO LONGER
   THELMA.
PLEASE SHOW ME HOW
   PAPA DU.
CAN'T YOU FEEL MY LOVE GROW STRONGER
   THELMA.
WITH YOUR ARMS AROUND ME TIGHT
   PAPA DU.
LOOKING IN YOUR EYES SO BRIGHT
   THELMA.
MY LOVE'S COMPLETE
   BOTH.
HONEY WHEN YOU KISS ME SWEET
(*Band and Dance*)
   PAPA DU.
IF THIS GONNA KILL ME LET YOUR SWEET PAPA DIE
   THELMA.
KISS ME NOW . . .
LOOKING IN YOUR EYES SO BRIGHT
HONEY WHEN YOU KISS ME SWEET

(*End of song they kiss* C.S. *and exit* US.C.)

Scene 2

(*PAPA DU enters, crossing to his chair. MA REED is seated in her chair.*)

PAPA DU. Aww, what you know?
BERTHA. (*enters in a rage*) Man, what did I tell you people. I sing that song and ain't nobody in this motherless show gonna do my stuff, (*THELMA enters with fan in right hand. BERTHA grabs fan.*) and right in front of my face. (*THELMA exits back dressing room.*)
BERTHA. (*to PAPA DU*) Now everytime I turn my back you got some hot brown heffer (*hits PAPA DU on head with fan*) squeezin' in my space. (*At her dressing table she bends down looking in mirror, slams down flask and takes off hat.*)
PAPA DU. (*looking at BERTHA's behind.*) My dear that ain't gonna be no tight squeeze. (*BERTHA swings around on him, as he jumps up from his chair.*) For your information Agie and Edna ain't here and you just come draggin' yo'self up in here late.
BERTHA. That was my opening number.
PAPA DU. Well you got payin' customers sittin' out there waitin' on you.
BERTHA. Well let the mothers wait. Let 'em all wait. And when they git tired let 'em stand up stretch their legs and wait some mo'. (*sitting in her chair*) Now I been hearin' all over town that you an this lil heffer been up to no good and behind my back. (*seated*) Bertha, you are talkin' out your head like usual. Bertha, you better git yo'self ready. (*BERTHA takes a swig from flask.*) Bertha I said to git ready. (*BERTHA takes another swig.*) Alright, Thelma . . . Thelma. (*THELMA appears in door to back dressing room.*) You go and sing another song baby. Go ahead.
THELMA. (*crossing to her chair*) If that's what you want 'cause you know whatever you want Papa Du I got to give it to ya.
BERTHA. (*rising and turning on THELMA*) This is still Bertha Williams company and I'm gonna do a number.
THELMA. But . . .
BERTHA. Sit yo butt down. (*THELMA sits*) And see, you, Mr. Too Hot to Trot . . . (*to PAPA DU*) I ain't blind, you know, but if I ever catch you two both of you gonna wish your mama never

let you out. (*exits to the stage as lights Blackout*) Git out of my way (*off stage to THEATRE OWNER*) (*entering US.C. stopping at piano*) "Don't turn your back on me."

PIANO PLAYER. (*to BERTHA, rising*) Now Bertha you know that ain't the next number.

BERTHA. (*banging on the piano lid with her hand*) HIT IT. (*band jumps and plays immediately.*)

[MUSIC #4: *DON'T TURN YOUR BACK ON ME*]

NEXT DOOR LAST NIGHT, ANOTHER FIGHT,
A MAN AND WIFE WERE AT IT ONCE MORE;
RIGHT THRU THE WALL, I HEARD IT ALL,
THESE WORDS/SHE LOUDLY/DID SPOKE:

AW, LOOK HERE PAPA/DON'T TURN YOUR BACK ON ME,
WHY MY KITTEN AND MY PUP/WOULD BE MORE COMPANY;
YOU JUST DON'T KNOW/THE PROPER WAY/TO TREAT A WIFE,
IN THE CEMETARY I COULD FIND MORE LIFE;
NOW, YOU'RE GETTING LAZY, ALL YOU DO IS SHIRK,
YOU HAD YOUR VACATION, NOW GET BACK TO WORK;
SHOW ME SOME AMBITION/OR GIVE IN YOUR KEY,
AND DON'T YOU TURN YOUR BACK ON ME.

(*Burlesque Routine*)
AW, LOOK HERE PAPA DON'T TURN YOUR BACK ON ME,
CAUSE IT AIN'T NEVER BEEN YOUR SHOULDER BLADES YOUR MAMA WANTS TO SEE
SAY WHILE A LADY'S SPEAKING/HONEY, DON'T YOU KNOW YOUR PLACE,
HOW CAN I GET RESULTS/IF I CAN'T SEE YOUR FACE;
GET ON OUT THERE IN THE STABLE/WITH THEM OTHER MULES,
CAUSE IT'S TOO DARN HOT TO TRY TO BE SO COOL,
COME ON, AND TREAT YOUR MAMA/WITH SOME DECENCY,
AND DON'T YOU TURN YOUR BACK ON ME,

TURN OVER HERE I SAID,
DON'T YOU TURN YOUR BACK ON ME.

Scene 3

(*THELMA and PAPA DU seated, MA REED is in backstage dressing room. BERTHA enters with the THEATRE OWNER right behind her.*)

Theatre Owner. Now Bertha. . . .
Bertha. (*turning on THEATRE OWNER*) I told you to stay out of my way. (*THEATRE OWNER backs out the door and she slams it.*)
Ma Reed. (*entering from backstage dressing room*) Oh. Come on now baby, come on. (*takes BERTHA's cape and hangs it up*) Now you know we got a show to do tonight. (*BERTHA sits.*) This is ridiculous. Why I seen more life in a whorehouse on a Sunday mornin and ya all know them folks be tired. Ya all come on now. (*sits down*)
Papa Du. It's all Bertha's fault comin' up in here pushin' people around. She's drunk that's what her problem is.
Bertha. Well if I ain't I been cheated outta eight dollars. You ever seen me with a bigger load than I can carry?
Papa Du. (*rises, takes jacket from rack and brushes it*) I seen you when I thought ya should a carried yo' load in two trips.
Bertha. Well, today was my New Orleans man's birthday and I decided to surprise him.
Papa Du. Whad ya do? Tell em your age?
Thelma. (*laughs, then turns to BERTHA laughing. BERTHA's stern look stops her laugh.*)
Bertha. (*to PAPA DU*) You askin' for it, ain't ya.
Papa Du. I ain't the one got to ask fo it.
Bertha. Course you don't. You wouldn't know what to do with even half of it.
Papa Du. Well you ain't never complained before. (*throws brush down and exits back stage dressing room*)
Ma Reed. (*jumping up in front of BERTHA*) Now y'all just cut that out. Lord have mercy. (*peeking after PAPA DU, tiptoes back to BERTHA*) Now tell me honey how was the black Rudolph Vaselino. Child I ain't seen that nigger in years.
Bertha. Well, he's fine now. (*Rubbing her chest provocatively;*

both ladies laugh.) Said things just ain't been shakin for him lately.

MA REED. Well like they always say honey. Blessed are those that expect nothin', for they shall not be disappointed. (*Both laugh as MA REED exits and lights fade.*)

[MUSIC #5: *JENNY'S BALL*]

THERE'S A MAN IN TOWN WHO'S CALLED THE LADY'S LOVER NOW
KEEPS HIS POCKETS FULL OF MIRRORS, HE'S THE TOP BOW WOW
HE WENT INTO A CABARET TO SEE MISS JENNY DANCE
JENNY STEPPED RIGHT UP, AND SAID YOU HAVE NO CHANCE
THERE'LL BE NO DOINGS HERE BEFORE YOU PAY
NO DANCING, PRANCING TILL THE BREAK OF DAY
I KNOW THERE'S LOTS OF GIRLIES YOU MAY CHARM
AND LONG TO HOLD THEM CLOSE UP, RIGHT IN YOUR ARMS
BUT HERE'S A LESSON THAT WAS TAUGHT TO ME
YOU CANNOT EAT AND SLEEP ON MIRTH AND GLEE
SO GOODBYE, AND PLEASE, DON'T CALL AT ALL
THERE'LL BE NO FREEBIES AT MISS JENNY'S BALL
EVERYTIME I STEP UP ON THAT BALLROOM FLOOR
THERE'S A CERTAIN FELLOW HERE WHO ASKS FOR MORE
I SEE I GOTTA GET YOU TOLD
BECAUSE YOU ACTING MIGHTY BOLD
SWEET PAPA, PROPER TALKING MAN
NOW BRING YOUR BUCKS AND BUCKS A PLENTY, HERE'S MY HAND
I'LL TAKE FROM A DOLLAR, FROM A DOLLAR TO A QUARTER
QUARTER TO A FRYING PAN
I NEED YOU, INDEED I DO
I GOT NO TIME TO BILL AND COO
THERE'LL BE NO FREEBIES AT MISS JENNY'S BALL.

(*Dance*)
BUT HERE'S A LESSON THAT WAS TAUGHT TO ME

YOU CANNOT EAT AND SLEEP ON MIRTH AND GLEE
SO GOODBYE AND PLEASE DON'T CALL AT ALL
THERE'LL BE NO FREEBIES AT MISS JENNY'S BALL.

Scene 4

(BERTHA, PAPA DU and THELMA seated.)

Ma Reed. *(entering)* Child, them folks is hot tonight. *(yelling into backstage dressing room)* Edna. Where is that slut? *(pose back stage dressing room)*

Thelma. Where ya think she's at. In jail. *(to BERTHA)*

Bertha. Well, that's what she gits tryin' to hustle a train conductor.

Ma Reed. *(sits)* I saw him takin' her off but I thought you said you was goin' to git her out.

Bertha. Well, I sent Agie down to the court house since four o'clock this afternoon with one hundred dollars in cash.

Papa Du. *(crossing out)* An' I told you don't trust that ol' ugly bugger bat with the money. *(exits to stage)*

Thelma. Well kids *(rising and picks up boa)* I saw Agie around sunset when I was comin' out the grocery. Had some luggage with him, tried to tell me it was his uncle's and he had to go git him out the hospital. *(To BERTHA; she exits to stage laughing.)*

Bertha. *(rises, takes cape and exits on line)* Well, if I find him, he's gonna keep that uncle of his company for a long time in that hospital . . . thievin ol possum faced fool. *(slams door in MA REED's face)*

Ma Reed. Lawd Lawd lawd. *(exits to stage)*

[music #6: *CAKE-WALKING BABIES FROM HOME*]

CAKE-WALKERS MAY COME,
CAKE-WALKERS MAY GO,
BUT I WANNA TELL YOU 'BOUT THIS COUPLE I KNOW.
THEY HIGH-STEPPIN' GALS,
AND DEBONAIR.
WHEN IT COMES TO BUSINESS NOT A SOUL CAN
  COMPARE.
Chorus.
HERE THEY COME,

LOOK AT 'EM DEMONSTRATIN',
GOING SOME,
LOOK AT 'EM SYNCOPATIN',
TALK OF THE TOWN,
EASIN' AROUND,
PICKIN 'EM UP,
AND LAYIN 'EM DOWN.
DANCING FOOLS,
THAT'S WHAT THEY LIKE TO CALL 'EM,
THEY'RE IN A CLASS OF THEIR OWN,
THE ONLY WAY FOR THEM TO LOSE IS TO CHEAT
  'EM,
YOU MAY TRY BUT YOU'LL NEVER BEAT 'EM.
STRUT YO' STUFF,
THEY DON'T DO NOTHIN' DIFF'RENT,
CAKE-WALKING BABIES FROM HOME.

DANCING FOOLS,
THAT'S WHAT THEY LIKE TO CALL 'EM,
THEY'RE IN A CLASS OF THEIR OWN.
THE ONLY WAY FOR THEM TO LOSE IS TO CHEAT
  'EM,
YOU MAY TRY BUT YOU'LL NEVER BEAT 'EM.
STRUT YO' STUFF,
THEY DON'T DO NOTHIN' DIFF'RENT,
CAKE-WALKING BABIES FROM HOME.

Scene 5

(*Right after CAKE-WALKING BABIES, PAPA DU enters first followed by THELMA and then MA REED who sit.*) Well ain't this just lovely. Agie done vacated with the money Edna's still in the jailhouse and Bertha ain't here again. Now I got to do Agie's ol' tired routine.

MA REED. (*with bread and mayonnaise*) You want a mayonnaise sandwich darlin'?
PAPA DU. Thelma, you go do "I got what it takes." Ma, you follow her. I got to go do Agies ol' tired routine. (*exits into backstage dressing room*)
THELMA. (*laughing, crosses to rack and takes cape with purse*

and gloves in other hand) Cute Papa Du goin' out there to do Agies routine. (*yelling to backstage dressing room*) Lawd, this I got to see. (*exits to stage*)

    MA REED. (*yelling, having eaten half the sandwich*) Do ya or don't ya want this mayonnaise sandwich?

    PAPA DU. (*appears in back dressing room doorway*) Ma. Why don't you just sit on that mayonnaise sandwich and slide. (*Blackout*)

[MUSIC #7: *I'VE GOT WHAT IT TAKES*]

OLE STINGY JENNY SAVED UP ALL HER PENNIES
STRAIGHT TO THE BANK SHE WOULD GO
THE SHARKS WOULD HOUND HER AND
  SURROUND HER
BUT NONE COULD GET HER DOUGH
JENNY'S FELLOW WAS A SLICK HIGH YELLOW
WHO WENT TO JAIL ONE DAY
HE CRIED FOR BAIL THEN TURNED REAL PALE
WHEN HE HEARD JENNY SAY
I GOT WHAT IT TAKES BUT IT BREAKS MY HEART
  TO GIVE IT AWAY
THESE STINGY MEN THEY CRYING FOR IT EVERY
  DAY
I BEEN SAVING IT UP FOR SUCH A LONG, LONG TIME
TO GIVE IT AWAY WOULD BE MORE THAN A CRIME
YOUR EYES MAY ROLL AND YOUR TEETH MAY GRIT
BUT NONE OF MY MONEY WILL YOU GET
YOU CAN LOOK IN MY BANK BOOK, BUT YOU
  BETTER NEVER PUT YOUR
HANDS ON MY PURSE (*Keep your hands off*)
'CAUSE I'M ONE WOMAN BELIEVES IN SAFETY
  FIRST, SAFETY FIRST
NOW IF YOU WANT MY MONEY, HERE'S MY PLAN
I AIN'T SAVING IT UP FOR NO STINKIN' MAN
I GOT WHAT IT TAKES BUT IT BREAKS MY HEART
  TO GIVE IT AWAY.

[MUSIC #8: *SEE SEE RIDER*]

I'M SO UNHAPPY
I FEEL SO BLUE

I ALWAYS FEEL SO SAD
I MADE A MISTAKE RIGHT FROM THE START
IT SEEMS SO HARD TO PART
ABOUT THIS LETTER
THAT I WILL WRITE
I HOPE HE WILL REMEMBER WHEN HE RECEIVES
 IT . . .

C.C. RIDER, SEE WHAT YOU DONE DONE
LAWD, LAWD, LAWD, MADE ME LOVE YOU
NOW YOUR GAL DONE COME
YOU MADE ME LOVE YOU
NOW YOUR GAL DONE COME
WELL I'M GWINE AWAY BABY
WON'T BE BACK TILL FALL
LAWD, LAWD, LAWD, GWINE AWAY BABY
WON'T BE BACK TILL FALL
IF I FIND ME A GOOD MAN
I WON'T BE BACK AT ALL
I'M GONNA BUY ME A PISTOL
JUST AS LONG AS I AM TALL
LAWD, LAWD, LAWD, KILL MY MAN AND
CATCH THAT CANNON BALL
IF HE WON'T HAVE ME
THEN HE WON'T HAVE NO GAL AT ALL

Scene 6

(*THELMA seated, PAPA DU in backstage dressing room.*)

THELMA. You better hurry up.
PAPA DU. (*entering in blackface*) I know, I know.
THELMA. Child you takes the cake.
MA REED. (*PAPA DU exits as she enters. When door shuts she laughs hysterically.*) Girl, did you see that mess?
PAPA DU. (*opens door*) What the hell you laughin' at? (*to MA REED*) You look like this all the time.

[MUSIC #9: *HE'S IN THE JAILHOUSE NOW*]

PAPA DU.
NOW UP IN NEW YORK CITY

FOLKS THOUGHT IT WAS A PITY
THAT THE LANDLORD HAD TO RAISE THAT
  RENT SO HIGH
WE HUSTLED 'ROUND THAT TOWN
IN ALL OUR HUSTLING 'ROUND
WE COULD NOT RAISE THAT RENT NO WAY WE TRIED
WELL MY MAMA TOOK IN WASHIN'
MY SISTER DONE THE IRONIN'
I HELPED AROUND THE TOWN BY SHININ' SHOES
BUT MY DADDY WALKED AROUND
LIKE HE OWNED NEW YORK TOWN
SPENDIN' ALL MAMA'S MONEY ON MOONSHINE
  BOOZE —
HE'S IN THE JAILHOUSE NOW
HE'S IN THE JAILHOUSE NOW
AND IF HE EVER GIT THAT RENT
CALL LONG DISTANCE TO REPENT
HE'S IN THE JAILHOUSE NOW —
NOW I WENT OUT LAST FRIDAY
I MET THIS BIG FAT GIRL NAMED IDA
WHO THOUGHT I WAS THE SWELLEST COON IN TOWN
SHE COMMENCED TO CALL ME HONEY
NATURALLY I BEGINS TO SPEND MY MONEY
WE TOOK IN EVERY CABARET COULD BE FOUND
WE WAS DRINKIN' EVERY MINUTE
I THOUGHT I WAS IN IT
WE WAS ORDERING JAMAICA RUM BY THE POUND
BUT WHEN I WENT TO PAY THAT MAN
I FOUND LIL IDA'S HAND
RIGHT IN MY POCKET WHERE MY MONEY WAS —
SHE'S IN THE GRAVEYARD NOW
SHE'S IN THE GRAVEYARD NOW
I TOLD THAT JUDGE RIGHT TO HIS FACE
IDA'S HANDS WAS OUT OF PLACE
SHE'S IN THE GRAVEYARD NOW.

Scene 7

(*MA REED, THELMA seated.*)

PAPA DU. Now look here Bertha. I don't appreciate what you just made me go out there and do. (*throws flag on back table*)

BERTHA. And what did I just make you go out there and do, Mr. Sambo. (*All laugh except PAPA DU.*)

PAPA DU. Did you git in touch with Agie's uncle? You call up that hospital?

BERTHA. The hospital seems to feel he ain't got no uncle. Seems he ain't got no family. In fact it seems to me he was born off the mold of an ol' piece of slimy bread.

PAPA DU. (*seated*) Which all goes to say that he's gone and the money too, huh?

BERTHA. Which all goes to say I ain't gonna sit around here wastin' my life worryin' about it. (*picks up flask and hands it to PAPA DU*) Now here. Have yo'self a hit of good ol' forgive 'em an forget 'em, dead or alive.

MA REED. (*as BERTHA exits to backstage dressing room*) You got it darlin', hallelujah for you, yes indeed.

BERTHA. (*exiting*) Alright Ma.

PAPA DU. Hey, Miss Amen Corner over there, when you goin' on stage?

MA REED. When I get myself prettied up.

PAPA DU. Child forgit it. You just go on out there. They think you either an ugly woman or a pretty monkey. (*THELMA laughs and exits to stage. MA laughs and exits to back dressing room.*)

MA REED. (*reentering and pointing at PAPA DU*) You got a bad attitude (*Blackout*)

[MUSIC #10: HE'S FUNNY THAT WAY]

THELMA.
HE SHOULD HAVE THE VERY BEST, THAT ANYONE CAN SEE
STILL HE'S DIFFERENT FROM ALL THE REST, SATISFIED WITH ME
THOUGH I WORRY, PLAN AND SCHEME, OVER WHAT TO DO
CAN'T HELP FEELING, IT'S A DREAM, AND TOO GOOD TO BE TRUE

I'M NOT MUCH TO LOOK AT, NOTHING TO SEE
I'M GLAD I'M LIVING AND LUCKY TO BE
I GOT A MAN, CRAZY FOR ME HE'S FUNNY THAT WAY
CAN'T SAVE A DOLLAR, AND HE AIN'T WORTH A CENT
HE DOESN'T HOLLER, WE LIVE IN A TENT
I GOT A MAN, CRAZY FOR ME AND HE'S FUNNY

THAT WAY
THOUGH HE LOVES TO WORK AND SLAVE FOR
  ME EVERYDAY
HE'D BE SO MUCH BETTER OFF, IF I WENT AWAY

BUT WHY SHOULD I LEAVE HIM, WHY SHOULD I GO
HE'D BE UNHAPPY WITHOUT ME I KNOW
I GOT A MAN WHO'S CRAZY FOR ME AND HE'S
  FUNNY THAT WAY

(*Over applause MA REED enters* US.R. *and crosses to* US.R.)

MA REED. And now ladies and gents the cutest boys on the block our band the Blue Serenaders (*exiting* US.C) Alright, hit it.

[MUSIC #11: *TIGER RAG*] (*Band solo*)

(*Band ends standing, then sits.*)

PAPA DU. (*entering* US.C. *gives band a bow if called for*) And now ladies and whatever you dragged in here with ya. Our own sweet singer of spiritual and secular ditties will now interpret "I can't do without my kitchen man" a song that reminds me of a poem my alcoholic aunt used to tell me while breathin' me to sleep.
Mary had a little lamb
her father killed it dead
now it goes to school with her
between two hunks of bread
Our own Bertha Williams as Madame Bux. (*gesters up* S.R.)

[MUSIC #12: *KITCHEN MAN*]

BERTHA.
MADAME BUX WAS QUITE DELUXE, SERVANTS
  BY THE SCORE
FOOTMEN AT EACH DOOR, AND BUTLERS AND
  MAIDS GALORE
BUT ONE DAY DAN HER KITCHEN MAN
GAVE IN HIS NOTICE HE'S THROUGH
SHE CRIED "OH DAN, DON'T LEAVE. IT'LL GRIEVE
  ME IF YOU DO."

HER HUSBAND ASKED HER WHY
AND THIS WAS HER REPLY:
I LOVE HIS CABBAGE, CRAVE HIS HASH
DAFFY ABOUT HIS SUCCATASH
I CAN'T DO WITHOUT MY KITCHEN MAN
WILD ABOUT HIS TURNIP TOPS
LIKES THE WAY HE WARMS MY CHOPS
I CAN'T DO WITHOUT MY KITCHEN MAN
NOW ANYBODY ELSE COULD LEAVE AND I
  WOULD ONLY LAUGH
'CAUSE HE MEANS SO MUCH TO ME, AND LISTEN
  HONEY
YOU AIN'T HEARD THE OTHER HALF
HIS JELLY ROLL IS SO NICE AND HOT
NEVER FAILS TO TOUCH THE SPOT
I CAN'T DO WITHOUT MY KITCHEN MAN
HIS FRANKFURTERS ARE OH SO SWEET
HOW I LOVE HIS SAUSAGE MEAT
I CAN'T DO WITHOUT MY KITCHEN MAN
HOW THAT BOY CAN OPEN CLAMS
NO ONE ELSE CAN TOUCH MY HAMS
I CAN'T DO WITHOUT MY KITCHEN MAN
NOW WHEN I EAT HIS DOUGHNUT
ALL I LEAVE IS THE HOLE
AND ANYTIME HE WANTS TO
HE CAN USE MY SUGAR BOWL
HIS BOLOGNA IS REALLY WORTH A TRY
NEVER FAILS TO SATISFY
I CAN'T DO WITHOUT MY *KITCHEN* MAN

Scene 8

(*PAPA DU lies back across his chair, THELMA is smoking and MA REED in her chair. BERTHA enters and exits immediately into back dressing room.*)

THEATRE OWNER. Bertha (*off stage*) Bertha. (*enters and doesn't see her in room*) Bertha. (*aghast, looking in back room*)

BERTHA. Measley ol' hound (*appears in doorway clutching dress to her breasts*) I know you peeping through the wrong window.

PAPA DU. He's just lookin' for some raw talent Bertha.

BERTHA. Don't worry about my talent honey I'm makin a livin' off it.

PAPA DU. You'd make yourself a fortune if you sold it by the pound.

BERTHA. You keep runnin' that big mouth of yours' . . .

THEATRE OWNER. Bertha, Bertha.

BERTHA. What, what.

THEATRE OWNER. You supposed to have six people in yo' company I ain't seen but four. Now you know this nullifies (*MA REED starts giggling.*) our contract agreement and you have all been notified thereof.

THELMA. You ain't notifyin' me of nothin' (*turns to PAPA DU*) you the company manager don't just sit there, say somethin'.

MA REED. Nullified thereof (*laughing*) Now what dat mean? (*turning to PAPA DU*)

PAPA DU. Dat mean he ain't gonna pay you.

MA REED. Don't play with me now (*gets up and paces dressing room*) You look here honey I got an uncle in heaven, an aunt in hell and a twin in prison. And if I don't get my money both of us is gonna visit one of 'em tonight.

THEATRE OWNER. (*backing into doorway*) Now just a minute you ain't supposed to talk to me that way.

MA REED. (*advancing on him*) Don't tell me how to talk you talkin' about my money. (*He runs out door and she chases him, stopped only by PAPA DU who grabs her arm and pulls her back into the dressing room.*)

PAPA DU. I'll handle it. (*exits*)

MA REED. (*paces dressing room then turns to THELMA*) Girl . . . Don't you know I got bad nerves.

THELMA. Go on and git 'em then.

MA REED. I know I should (*charges out door*)

THEATRE OWNER. (*darting through the curtain addressing the piano player*) Play something. . . .

MA REED. (*darts through curtain grabs him around waist and drags him off*) Come back here and talk about the money.

THEATRE OWNER. (*being dragged off*) Quiiiiick.

(*Trumpet player crosses* DS.C. *with vintage stand mike and sings.*)

SHAKE THAT THING

(*End of number. Trumpet player crosses up stage with mike.*)

[MUSIC #13: *WAIT TILL YOU SEE MY BABY DO THE CHARLESTON*]

JUST WAIT TILL YOU SEE MY BABY DO THE
  CHARLESTON DANCE
JUST WAIT TILL YOU SEE MY BABY DO THE
  CHARLESTON PRANCE
THE WAY THEY DO IT IN NEW YORK IS SIMPLY
  FINE, MIGHTY FINE
BUT IT DON'T COMPARE TO THAT SWEET MAN
  OF MINE, FROM SOUTH CAROLINA
JUST WAIT TILL YOU SEE MY BABY DO THE
  CHARLESTON STRUT
OH WAIT TILL YOU SEE MY BABY DO NOTHIN'
  ELSE BUT
THERE HE GOES ON HIS TOES
WHERE HE LEARNED IT NO ONE KNOWS
JUST WAIT TILL YOU SEE MY BABY DO THE
  CHARLESTON DANCE
JUST WAIT TILL YOU SEE MY BABY DO THE
  CHARLESTON DANCE (STEP ON IT HONEY)
JUST WAIT TILL YOU SEE MY BABY DO THE
  CHARLESTON PRANCE (READY FOR THE MONEY)
THE WAY THEY DO IN NEW YORK IS SIMPLY
  FINE, MIGHTY FINE
BUT IT DON'T COMPARE TO THAT SWEET MAN
  OF MINE, FROM SOUTH CAROLINA
JUST WAIT TILL YOU SEE MY BABY DO THE
  CHARLESTON STRUT (BLACK BOTTOM BABY)
OH WAIT TILL YOU SEE MY BABY DO NOTHIN'
  ELSE BUT (DON'T MEAN MAYBE)
THERE HE GOES ON HIS TOES
WHERE HE LEARNED IT NO ONE KNOWS
JUST WAIT TILL YOU SEE MY BABY DO THE
  CHARLESTON DANCE

(*MA REED dance*)

MA REED.
MAN OF MINE
  THELMA.
FROM CAROLINE

BERTHA.
MIGHTY FINE
ALL.
HE'S MINE ALL MINE

(*Blackout*)

THEATRE OWNER. (*enters* US.C. *in spotlight*) Well we'll just cut it right here and give these folks a breather. And whoever stuffed all that tissue paper down the latrine in the men's facilities have inconvenienced yourselves as much as me. So gentlemen, use the wall buckets only. And remember if you go out of the theatre keep your ticket stubs 'cause if you don't you ain't gettin back in. Oh, speakin' of ticket stubs the winner of tonight's door prize is holdin' ticket number (*He reaches in pocket and pulls out ticket. Drum rolls loudly, covering his voice as he reads number; cymbal crash on his exit.*)

ACT TWO

[MUSIC #14: *ENTR'ACTE: MUSKRAT RAMBLE*]

THEATRE OWNER. Alright. Y'all done had enough time out there. Can't be lollygagging around here all night. Barney, shut the door. (*The house door slams.*) If they ain't back in their seats by now — tough.)

[MUSIC #15: *BLACK BOTTOM*]

(*Piano and drums roll. MA REED enters staggering US.R. and crosses C.S. Piano and drums continue to roll. She signals for them to stop, but they continue. Finally, she kicks her foot at pianist, who stops.*)

MA REED.
ON THE BLACK BOTTOM OF THE SWANEE RIVER
SOMETIMES LIKE TO SHAKE AND SHIVER
AND IT MAKES THE DARKIES FEEL LIKE
 STRUTTIN AROUND
BY WATCHING, THEY FOUND A WAY TO IMITATE IT
I KNOW THEY AGGRAVATE IT
BUT I WISH THAT YOU COULD SEE THE DANCE
 THAT THEY FOUND
ALL THE HIGH BROWN GALS AND THEIR BON
 BON BUDDIES
GO DOWN WHERE THE FLATS ARE MUDDY TO
 DO THE DANCE THAT SOON WILL BE
REKNOWN . . . THEY CALL IT BLACK BOTTOM
A NEW TWISTER, THEY SURE GOT 'EM AND OH
 SISTER
THEY CLAP THEIR HANDS AND DO A RAGGEDY
 TROT (AND MAN IT'S HOT)
OLE FELLOWS WITH LUMBAGO, AND HIGH
 YELLOWS AWAY THEY GO
THEY JUMP RIGHT IN AND GIVE IT ALL THAT
 THEY GOT
THEY SAY THAT WHEN THAT RIVER BOTTOMS
 COVERED WITH OOZE
(START IN TO SQUIRM)

YOUNG FOLKS DANCE AND THAT'S THE
  MOVEMENT THEY USE
(JUST LIKE A WORM)
BLACK BOTTOM A NEW RHYTHM, WHEN YOU
  SPOT 'EM YOU GO WITH 'EM
AND DO THAT BLACK BLACK BOTTOM ALL THE
  DAY LONG

Scene 9

(*THELMA sprays BERTHA's perfume MA REED enters. BERTHA and MA REED sit.*)

MA REED. Girl, this work is too hard for that man to be messin' with my money.

(*PAPA DU enters.*)

BERTHA. You sure about that contract?

PAPA DU. Will y'all just let me handle the business. Now the contract ain't said nothin' about six people. It said four singers, an exotic dancer, and a blackface comedian. (*over BERTHA's shoulder*) Thanks to you everyone out there tonight know'd they done seen a blackface comedian. Now all we need is an exotic dancer appearance then we got what you call yourself a "loophole." (*crosses to THELMA*) Now if this pretty lil filly here would do her fellow performers a service —

THELMA. Look man, you must have loopholes in your brain.

PAPA DU. Thelma, I explained all that . . .

THELMA. You must be a fool. Now I told you twice I ain't doin it. What do I have to do to make myself plain?

MA REED. Nothin'. (*rises at her place*) The Lord already took care of that. (*exits through door but stopped half way out by THELMA*)

THELMA. I bet you won't be laughin' when you don't git your money.

MA REED. And I bet you won't be laughin' when I (*three steps towards THELMA raising arm to strike her*) Whip yo aaaa—

BERTHA. (*rises, grabbing MA by the waist and upraised arm*) Alright. (*wrestling MA out the door*) Now I done handled bigger problems than this snotty-nosed prima donna.

Papa Du. (*to THELMA*) Now look. There's an extra dollar and a quarter in it.
Ma Reed. (*opens door and pops her head in*) Oh yeah. (*starts entering to sit*)
Papa Du. (*to MA, pointing out door*) Not you. (*MA exits grumbling. Crossing to door, he turns back to THELMA.*) Come on, Thelma. Do the skit. You can still do that huh? (*Lights fade as party vamp starts. ALL enter* US.C.)

[MUSIC #16: *TAKE IT ON OUTTA HERE*]

(*BERTHA enters.*)

Bertha. Ladies and Gentleman . . . The Party! (*MA REED, PAPA DU enter. Knock at the door.*)
Ma Reed. Somebody answer the door.
Bertha. I'm going . . .
Ma Reed. Well, I wish you'd gone on then.
Papa Du. I wish you'd stop spittin' them potato chips in my face!

(*THELMA enters*)

Bertha. What you want to invite her here for?
Thelma. You don't want me here?
Bertha. Shhhhh . . .
Thelma. Don't shush me! I'm as nice as anybody in town.
Bertha. Where did you get drunk at?
Thelma. EVERYWHERE! And who don't like it, hey, hey!
Bertha. Well go right back where you got drunk at 'cause if you stay here, I'm gonna have to get you told.
Thelma. Ain't nothin' you can tell me Big Mama!
Bertha. Now look like you trying to take advantage of me lil ole gal from the South!
Thelma. (How?)
Bertha. Everytime I give a party, you come up here and try to turn it out.
Thelma. (Oh no I don't.)
Bertha. And you go down and get your friend Hattie Brown you know who I'm talking about.
Thelma. (Yeah.)

BERTHA. And she don't do nothin' but low rate my friends down to the ground.

THELMA. Well, I tell you the reason I do it Miss "Uptown Ann."

BERTHA. (Why?)

THELMA. 'Cause you so dirty, look like you try to take everybody's man.

BERTHA. (Now that's a lie.) Come on Ma, git up on outta that chair. (*Pulls her up*)

MA REED. For what?

BERTHA. 'Cause where you go from here, honey, you know I really don't care.

BERTHA. (*sings*)
JUST SO YOU TAKE IT ON OUTTA HERE.
BEFORE I HIT YOU IN THE HEAD WITH THIS CHAIR
THELMA. (YOU BETTER STAND READY.)
BERTHA. (*sings*)
NOW DON'T BE AROUND WHEN MY TEMPER RISE
THELMA. (I AIN'T STEDDIN 'BOUT YOUR TEMPER!)
BERTHA. (sings)
'CAUSE WHAT I'LL PUT ON YOU WILL BE A SURPRISE.
THELMA. (Maybe)
BERTHA. (sings)
NOW IF YOU DON'T GO, YOU'LL WISH YOU HAD WENT.
I'M THE BOSS OF THIS DUMP
I'M THE ONE THAT PAYS THE RENT
TAKE IT ON OUTTA HERE, HOT MAMA
I DON'T WANT IT HERE.

MA REED. (Nah how come you don't want me here?)

BERTHA. Now the reason I don't want you here, cause you so doggone cheap.

MA REED. (Cheap?)

BERTHA. You brought one ole half pint of liquor and don't want to part with it!

MA REED. (That's what you say) . . .

BERTHA. You been bumming for six months, on nothin' but liquor and beer.

MA REED. (Yeah!)

BERTHA. Now you know hot mama why I don't want you here.

MA REED. Yeah you serve that ole no-good liquor.

ONE MO' TIME

BERTHA. (What no-good liquor.)
MA REED. And that ole rotten beer.
BERTHA. (I made this beer myself.)
MA REED. But child when I get through snitching on you the police gonna have to move you from here. You went next door and talked about me to Elizabeth.
THELMA. (Sure did.)
MA REED. But I'm gonna put goffer dust through your keyhole and make you sneeze yourself to death.
BERTHA. Yeah you start to hoo-dooing on me I got something I'll do.
MA REED. (What is it?)
BERTHA. I'll give you one more drink of my liquor and I'll poison you.
MA REED. (That's what you think.)
BERTHA. I got something right here that shoots ninety-nine times.
BERTHA. And when the first shot hit you, you gonna change your flipping mind.

(*ALL three sing.*)

SO TAKE IT ON OUTTA HERE.
TAKE IT ON OUTTA HERE!

[MUSIC #17: *HOP SCOP BLUES*]

OLE NEW ORLEANS IS A GREAT BIG OLE
  SOUTHERN TOWN
WHERE HOSPITALITY, IT CAN SURE BE FOUND
THE POPULATION THERE, IS VERY VERY FAIR
AND LORD THE THINGS THEY DO, WHITE FOLKS
  Y'ALL DO IT TO
THEY GOT A DANCE AND IT SURE IS SOMETHING
  RARE THERE
YOU GOT TO, GLIDE, SLIDE, PRANCE OH DANCE
HOP, STOP . . . TAKE IT EASY HONEY, YEAH. YEAH
I NEVER GET TIRED DANCING MY HOP SCOP BLUES
ONCE MO . . . YOU GOT TO GLIDE, SLIDE,
  PRANCE, DANCE
THAT HOP SCOP BLUES WILL MAKE YOU DO A

LOVELY SHAKE
AND MAKE YOU FEEL SO GRAND WHEN YOU
  WALK HAND IN HAND
I NEVER GOT TIRED OF DANCING MY HOP SCOP
  BLUES

(*Dance* C.S.—*PAPA DU*)

[MUSIC #18: *HINDUSTAN*]

(*MA REED enters* US.R. *and poses before crossing* D.S. *into exotic dance. End of number she bows several times and runs off* US.C.)

Scene 10

(*BERTHA, THELMA and PAPA DU are all sitting.*)

THEATRE OWNER. (*slams door open in a rage; said unbelievingly*) This is an outrage.
BERTHA. What did you mean (*MA REED enters; stops in door, then exits back stage dressing room giving the THEATRE OWNER a look over her shoulder.*) by that. (*points to MA*)
THELMA. And what do you mean "that" ain't no "that" back here.
THEATRE OWNER. Now you watch it. (*crossing to THELMA and pointing at her*)
PAPA DU. Bertha, don't worry yourself none cause legally he can't touch you child, you done had yourself a most exotic dancer.
THEATRE OWNER. (*leaning over BERTHA*) Well, if you think I'm gonna pay for that you got another think comin' and furthermore—
BERTHA. Look man (*rises, backing THEATRE OWNER towards door*) you asked for Bertha Williams and her tourin company (*She grabs him by jacket and raises him on his tiptoes. Both are parallel to the door.*) and you gittin' Bertha Williams and her tourin' company (*Crosses* S.L. *to PAPA DU*) minus a little bad company I been keepin lately.
MA REED. (*enters at BERTHA's left shoulder; to THEATRE OWNER*) Now look what you done gone and done.

THEATRE OWNER. What?
MA REED. (*patting BERTHA's shoulder*) Upsettin' that poor woman. (*She exits. BERTHA drops THEATRE OWNER and crosses D.S. of coat rack.*)
THEATRE OWNER. (*crossing to BERTHA, brushing down jacket*) Now now Bertha. You all are just doin' a fine (*patting her right shoulder and hand wanders to her breast*) fine job.
BERTHA. (*knocking hand off breast*) Wait a minute. You don't know me. You just can't see, can ya? (*backing THEATRE OWNER to door*) You just don't understand. (*slams door as THEATRE OWNER runs out, turns and addresses room*) See, it's like a family. (*PAPA DU hands her the flask.*) A flock. (*In front of her dressing table she takes a long swig from flask.*) Your own flock. (*puts bottle on table*) The people back here and the people out there. (*gestering to door*) It's like your own flock. And you look down and one of 'em done pissed on your foot. (*exits, blackout*)

[MUSIC #19: WHAT IT TAKES TO BRING YOU BACK]

(*PAPA DU enters US.C. with suitcase and crosses half way on stage. He looks back at curtain as BERTHA bursts through, in hot pursuit. He crosses DS.C. and puts down suitcase.*)

PAPA DU.
BERTHA IF I GO AWAY
 BERTHA.
THEN WHAT
 PAPA DU.
TELL ME WHAT YOU'RE GONNA DO
 BERTHA.
(SAY LISTEN), PAPA YOU'LL COME BACK SOMEDAY
 PAPA DU.
I WOULDN'T BE TOO SURE NOW
 BERTHA.
AND I WON'T BE BEGGIN' YOU
 PAPA DU.
HUH, BABY YOU SURE LOVE YOURSELF
 BERTHA.
SAY WHAT?
 PAPA DU.
NEVER HEARD SUCH BRAGGIN' SO

BERTHA.
SAY LISTEN, NOW CAN'T PUT ME ON NO SHELF
PAPA DU.
I CAN'T EVEN PICK YOU UP.
BERTHA.
SO WRITE THIS DOWN BEFORE YOU GO
PAPA DU.
WHAT IS THAT?
BERTHA. (*sings*)
WHAT IT TAKES TO BRING YOU BACK
YOUR MAMA KEEPS IT ALL THE TIME
PAPA DU.
YOU ALWAYS MAKING SOME OLE WISE CRACKS AND
YOU KNOW YOUR ONIONS AIN'T WORTH A DIME
BERTHA.
SAY LISTEN, DON'T THINK 'CAUSE I'M FAT MY LOVE
AIN'T GUARANTEED
PAPA DU.
IF I'M GONNA HANDLE ALL THAT
I BETTER GO SMOKE ME SOME WEED
BERTHA.
NOW WHAT IT TAKES TO BRING YOU BACK YOUR
MAMA KEEPS IT ALL THE TIME
PAPA DU.
I'M GONNA TRY SOME
BERTHA.
THEN YOU'LL WANT IT ALL THE TIME

(*Dance routine*)

BERTHA.
NOW WHAT IT TAKES TO BRING YOU BACK
YOUR MAMA KEEPS IT ALL THE TIME
PAPA DU.
WELL LOOK HERE MISS B., IF THAT'S A NATURAL
FACT ON YOUR MOVING VAN I'M GONNA CLIMB
BERTHA.
SAY LISTEN, I GOT SOMETHING IN MY MOVEMENT
THAT'S JUST TOO TIGHT
PAPA DU.
WELL IF YOU WANT TO KEEP ME MAMA, YOU BETTER
MOVE IT RIGHT

Bertha.
NOW WHAT IT TAKES TO BRING YOU BACK YOUR
  MAMA KEEPS IT ALL THE TIME
Papa Du.
I'M GONNA TRY SOME
Bertha.
THEN YOU'LL ALL THE TIME.

[music #20: *EVERYBODY LOVES MY BABY*]

I'M AS HAPPY AS CAN BE
CLEAR SKIES ARE ALL THAT I SEE
WHENEVER HE MAKES LOVE TO ME, I GOT TO
  LET IT OUT
HE'S MY SWEETIE CAN'T YOU GUESS
WILD ABOUT HIM I CONFESS
DOES HE LOVE ME, O MY YES, THAT'S JUST WHY
  I SHOUT
EVERYBODY LOVES MY BABY BUT MY BABY
  DON'T LOVE NOBODY BUT ME
NOBODY BUT ME
EVERYBODY WANTS MY BABY, BUT MY BABY
  DON'T WANT NOBODY BUT ME
THAT'S PLAIN TO SEE
HE'S GOT THOSE ELGIN MOVEMENTS TWENTY
  YEARS GUARANTEED
THERE'S NO NEED FOR IMPROVEMENT MY SWEET
  DADDY'S BUILT FOR SPEED
THAT'S WHY, EVERYBODY LOVES MY BABY, BUT
  MY BABY DON'T LOVE
NOBODY BUT ME, NOBODY BUT ME

(*Clarinet Solo*)
EVERYBODY LOVES MY BABY, BUT MY BABY
  DON'T LOVE NOBODY BUT ME
NOBODY BUT ME
EVERYBODY WANTS MY BABY, BUT MY BABY
  DON'T WANT NOBODY BUT ME
THAT'S PLAIN TO SEE
WHEN MY BABY KISSES ME UPON MY ROSY CHEEK
I JUST LET THOSE KISSES BE, DON'T WASH MY
  FACE FOR WEEKS

THAT'S WHY EVERYBODY LOVES MY BABY, BUT
  MY BABY DON'T LOVE NOBODY BUT ME
NOBODY BUT ME, YEAH

[MUSIC #21: *YOU'VE GOT THE RIGHT KEY BUT THE WRONG KEYHOLE*]

BERTHA.
NOW LIZA JOHNSON AND HER MAN,
HAD A FALLING OUT.
HE SAID GET SOMEONE ELSE IF YOU CAN,
'CAUSE I'M GONE WITHOUT A DOUBT.
THINGS GOT TOUGH AND HE CAME BACK,
LAST NIGHT ABOUT NINE O'CLOCK
HE PUT HIS KEY IN THE OLD FRONT DOOR,
BUT THE KEY DIDN'T FIT THE LOCK.
HE PUSHED IT IN,
AND TURNED IT 'ROUND,
AND 'ROUND THEN HE TOOK IT OUT.
AND JUST WHEN HE WAS 'BOUT TO TRY IT AGAIN,
HE HEARD MISS LIZA SHOUT:
  CHORUS.
YOU GOT THE RIGHT KEY BUT THE WRONG
  KEYHOLE,
I COULDN'T GET ALONG WITH YOU TO SAVE MY
  SOUL.
YESTERDAY I WENT DOWN TO THE HARDWARE
  STORE,
AND PUT ANOTHER LOCK ON MY FRONT DOOR.
I GOT A NEW MAN WHO IS BETTER THAN YOU,
HE STARTS HIS LOVING WHERE YOU GET THROUGH.
SO TAKE MY TIP HONEY AND LEAVE MY DOOR,
BECAUSE YOUR KEY DON'T FIT IN MY LOCK NO
  MORE,
I SAY YOU GOT THE RIGHT KEY,
BUT YOU'RE WORKING ON THE WRONG KEYHOLE

(*Strip Routine*)
I GOT A NEW MAN WHO IS BETTER THAN YOU,
HE STARTS HIS LOVING WHERE YOU GET THROUGH.
SO TAKE MY TIP HONEY AND LEAVE MY DOOR,
BECAUSE YOUR KEY DON'T FIT IN MY LOCK NO
  MORE,

I SAY YOU GOT THE RIGHT KEY,
BUT YOU'RE WORKING ON THE WRONG KEYHOLE.

[MUSIC #22: *AFTER YOU'VE GONE*]

MA REED.
NOW LISTEN HONEY WHILE I SAY
HOW CAN YOU TELL ME THAT YOU'RE GOING AWAY
DON'T SAY THAT WE MUST PART
DON'T BREAK MY ACHING HEART
YOU KNOW I LOVED YOU TRUE FOR MANY A YEAR
LOVED YOU NIGHT AND DAY
HOW CAN YOU LEAVE ME, CAN'T YOU SEE MY TEARS
SO LISTEN WHILE I SAY

AFTER YOU'VE GONE AND LEFT ME CRYING
AFTER YOU'VE GONE THERE'S NO DENYING
YOU'LL FEEL BLUE AND YOU'LL FEEL SAD
YOU'LL MISS THE DEAREST PAL THAT YOU EVER HAD
THERE'LL COME A TIME, WHEN YOU'LL REGRET IT.
THERE'LL COME A TIME, AND DON'T FORGET IT.
SOMEDAY WHEN YOU'VE GROWN LONELY
YOUR HEART WILL ACHE LIKE MINE AND YOU'LL
   WANT ME ONLY
AFTER YOU'VE GONE, AFTER YOU'VE GONE AWAY

(*Music release*)
SOMEDAY WHEN YOU'VE GROWN LONELY
YOUR HEART WILL ACHE LIKE MINE AND YOU'LL
   WANT ME ONLY
AFTER YOU'VE GONE, AFTER YOU'VE GONE AWAY

(*Blackout*)

SCENE 11

(*BERTHA is sitting, also PAPA DU who is playing cards by himself.*)

MA REED. (*enters excited*) Girl. (*to BERTHA*) Did you see that fine man out there in the second row?
BERTHA. I sho did. (*MA REED exits back stage. To THELMA*

who enters from the back stage dressing room and exits halfway out the door.) Where you goin honey?

THELMA. I'm goin to sing my song.

BERTHA. (*rises and crosses up by PAPA DU*) Well, I do believe my song is the next one up.

THELMA. (*steps into the room*) Well Papa Du told me I could try that song tonight, didn't ya?

PAPA DU. (*clearing his throat*) Now all I said was maybe, if Bertha didn't mind I was gonna ask her.

THELMA. (*advances to her chair*) Well Mr. hen pecked that ain't what you said last night.

BERTHA. (*crossing to THELMA's chair, leans on it and looks at PAPA DU*) Oh. So you gonna take my song and give it to your young stuff. Tell me what you gonna git for my song. (*laugh, bangs chair*) Come on tell me what you gonna git for it.

PAPA DU. (*rises*) Now Bertha, all I said was that it wasn't my place.

BERTHA. (*counter crossing PAPA DU to D.L.*) I do believe you done stepped outta your place and into trouble.

PAPA DU. (*holding her arms from behind her*) Now baby don't git yourself all upset.

BERTHA. (*struggling*) Upset.

THELMA. (*removes headband and feather and crossing to BERTHA*) Now look, you let me tell you one thing. You ain't wrote it. It's mine just like it is yours.

PAPA DU. (*struggling*) And you ain't gonna be satisfied till we carry you outta here in a dust pan. (*BERTHA bites his hand and he recoils to back stage doorway.*) Ooooow.

BERTHA. (*turning to THELMA*) You can't sing it no way.

THELMA. Why?

BERTHA. Cause you got a sore lip.

THELMA. I ain't got no sore lip.

BERTHA. Well you do now. (*BERTHA grabs THELMA's hair and they struggle. PAPA DU is U.S. in the middle.*)

THELMA. Let go. Let go my hair. You ole crazy woman. You crazy. (*BERTHA pulls off THELMA's wig and holds it in the air. Leaning on MA REED's chair.*) Well you just keep it then.

PAPA DU. (U.C., *stares at THELMA*) Lord have mercy. (*BERTHA starts to lunge for THELMA, but PAPA DU steps between and stops BERTHA.*) Now Bertha you know this woman always tryin' to start trouble.

BERTHA. She start it I'm gonna finish it, ok?

PAPA DU. No. (*BERTHA turns away D.S.*) Now c'mon Bertha.

(*Behind her he tries to put his arms around her, but she pushes them off.*) Bertha baby. (*He tries again but she pushes his hands away again. He straightens his tie, rubs his palms and this time succeeds in wrapping his arms around her waist, sings in her ear.*) What it takes to bring you back. Yo' Pappa keeps it (*leans back pushing his hips into her behind*) aaallll the time. (*BERTHA's head falls back on his shoulder.*)

THELMA. Disgustin'. (*dead pan*)

BERTHA. (*Crossing to THELMA, she taps her on the shoulder.*) Ha ha ha. (*exits to stage*)

PAPA DU. (*He wipes his brow, picks up wig from THELMA's table and crosses to door. Turning back to THELMA*) Now girl. All this time I thought you had good hair. (*THELMA grabs wig and flogs him with it as music begins and lights fade. He backs out door.*)

[MUSIC #23: *MY MAN BLUES*]

BERTHA.
THELMA. WHO WAS THAT MAN I SAW YOU WITH THE OTHER DAY
THELMA.
THAT DAY THAT WAS MY SMOOTH DADDY THAT WE CALL CHARLIE GRAY
BERTHA.
DON'T YOU KNOW THAT WAS MY MAN, YEAH THAT'S A FACT
THELMA.
I SEEN HIS NAME PRINTED UP AND DOWN YOUR BACK
BERTHA.
THAT'S MY MAN, I WANT HIM FOR MY OWN
THELMA.
(YOU GOT TO BE KIDDIN' HONEY)
HE'S MY SWEET DADDY AND YOU BETTER LEAVE THAT MAN ALONE
BERTHA.
WELL SEE THAT SUIT HE GOT ON, I BOUGHT IT FOR HIM LAST WEEK
THELMA.
I BEEN BUYING CLOTHES FOR TWO YEARS, COST ME ALL MY BACK GOLD TEETH

(*Knock*)

BERTHA.
IS THAT YOU HONEY
BERTHA.
SOUNDS LIKE MY MAN SWEET CHARLIE GRAY
THELMA.
YO' MAN, HOW DID HE GET THAT WAY
BERTHA.
WELL HE'S BEEN MY MAN FOR UMPTEEN YEARS
THELMA.
CHILE, DON'T YOU KNOW I'LL TURN YOUR DAPPER DOWN
BERTHA.
YES THELMA AND I'LL CUT YOU EVERY WAY BUT LOOSE
THELMA.
WELL YOU MIGHT AS WELL BEGIN IT THEN
BERTHA.
WELL THEN . . . (TOGETHER NOSE TO NOSE)
THELMA.
I GUESS WE GOT TO HAVE HIM ON COOPERATION PLAN
BERTHA.
I GUESS WE GOT TO HAVE HIM ON COOPERATION PLAN
TOGETHER.
BERTHA . . . THELMA . . . AIN'T NOTHING DIFFERENT, ALL WE GOT IS A TWO TIME MAN.

(Cross over. THELMA enters dressing room and sits at her table combing her wig. PAPA DU enters on a music cue, looking back over his shoulder in the doorway, then crosses to behind THELMA, talking in her ear. She turns from him sharply as MA REED enters. MA pulls PAPA DU by the shoulder and points to the door. PAPA DU exits.)

[MUSIC #24: *PAPA DE-DA-DA*]

PAPA DU.
DOWN IN NEW ORLEANS,
LAND OF DREAMY SCENES.
THERE'S A MAN,
MUSIC MAN,
PLAYS AND SINGS,
BUCK AND WINGS.
PAPA TREE TOP TALL,

WELL HE'S LONG AND LEAN THAT'S ALL.
EVERY NIGHT,
IT'S A SIGHT
YOU SHOULD HEAR FOLKS CALL.
  Chorus.
PAPA DE-DA-DA,
I'M THE LADIES MAN,
PAPA DE-DA-DA,
I CAN SING THE BLUES,
PAPA DE-DA-DA,
SWEETEST IN THE LAND,
PAPA DE-DA-DA,
WATCH HIM CLAP HIS HANDS,
HE CAN PLAY PIANO GRAND.
PAPA DE-DA-DA,
SPREAD THE LATEST NEWS.
SO NEAT AND KEEN,
THAT'S WHAT I MEAN,
GOT ALL THE GALS IN NEW ORLEANS.
PAPA DE, DA, DA-DA-DA,
HE'S THE HOTTEST MAN IN TOWN.
  (*PAPA DU dances.*)
PAPA DE-DA-DA,
I'M THE LADIES MAN,
PAPA DE-DA-DA,
SWEETEST IN THE LAND,
PAPA DE-DA-DA,
WATCH HIM CLAP HIS HANDS,
HE CAN PLAY PIANO GRAND.
PAPA DE-DA-DA,
I CAN SING THE BLUES,
PAPA DE-DA-DA,
SPREAD THE LATEST NEWS.
SO NICE AND SOFT,
HE NEVER SCOFFS.
OLE RED HOT MAMAS HE COOLS THEM OFF.
PAPA DE, DA, DA-DA-DA,
HE'S THE HOTTEST MAN IN TOWN.

    [music #25: *MUDDY WATERS*]

  Optional:
Ma Reed or Bertha.
DIXIE MOON LIGHT, SWANEE SHORE, HEADED

HOMEBOUND, JUST ONCE MORE
TO MY MISSISSIPPI DELTA HOME
SOUTHLAND HAS A GRAND GARDEN SPOT
ALTHOUGH YOU BELIEVE OR NOT
I HEAR THOSE TREES A WHISPERING
COME ON BACK TO ME
MUDDY WATERS ROUND MY FEET
MUDDY WATERS IN THE STREET
THAT'S GOD'S OWN SHELTER, DOWN ON THE DELTA
MUDDY WATERS IN MY SHOES
REELING AND ROCKING TO THEM LOW DOWN BLUES
THEY LIVE IN EASY COMFORT THERE, YEAH! I
  DO DECLARE
BEEN AWAY A YEAR TODAY, TO WANDER AND ROAM
I DON'T CARE IT'S MUDDY THERE, 'CAUSE STILL
  IT'S MY HOME
GOT MY TOES TURNED DIXIE WAY
ROUND THE DELTA LET ME LAY
MY HEART CRIES OUT FOR MUDDY WATERS

[MUSIC #26: ... *HOT TIMES IN THE OLE TOWN TONIGHT*]

COMPANY.
COME ALONG GET READY, WEAR YOUR BRAND
  BRAND NEW GOWN
'CAUSE THERE'S GONNA BE A MEETING IN THIS
  GOOD GOOD OLE TOWN
WHEN YOU KNOW EVERYBODY AND THEY ALL
  KNOW YOU
AND YOU GET A RABBIT'S FOOT TO KEEP AWAY
  THE HOO-DOO
WHEN YOU HEAR THAT THE PREACHING HAS BEGIN
BEND DOWN LOW FOR TO DRIVE AWAY YOUR SIN
WHEN YOU GET RELIGION YOU'LL WANT TO
  SHOUT AND SING
THERE'LL BE A HOT TIME, IN THE OLE TOWN
  TONIGHT
MY BABY. . . .
WHEN YOU HEAR THE BELLS GO DING-A-LING
ALL JOIN 'ROUND, AND SWEETLY YOU MUST SING
WHEN THE VERSE IS THROUGH, IN THE CHORUS

Y'ALL ALL JOIN IN
THERE'LL BE A HOT TIME, IN THE OLE TOWN,
TONIGHT

THERE'LL BE GIRLS FOR EVERYBODY IN THIS
 GOOD, GOOD OLE TOWN
THERE'S MISS GONZOLA DAVIS AND MISS
 GODZULA BROWN
THERE'S HENRIETTA BEEZER AND SHE'S ALL
 DRESSED-UP IN RED
WELL I JUST HUGGED AND KISSED HER AND TO
 ME THEN SHE SAID

PLEASE OH PLEASE, OH DO NOT LET ME GO
YOU ARE MINE, AND I LOVE YOU BEST OF ALL
YOU'LL BE MY MAN, OR I'LL HAVE NO MAN AT ALL
THERE'LL BE A HOT TIME IN THE OLE TOWN TONIGHT
MY BABY
WHEN YOU HEAR THE BELLS GO DING-A-LING
ALL JOIN 'ROUND, AND SWEETLY YOU MUST SING
WHEN THE VERSE IS THROUGH, IN THE CHORUS
 Y'ALL ALL JOIN IN
THERE'LL BE A HOT TIME, IN THE OLE TOWN,
TONIGHT

DANCE

(*After dance the COMPANY all bows*
The BAND bows after THEATRE OWNER enters U.R., *bows*
 and is followed by the TRUMPET PLAYER. All sing the
 ENCORE, bow and exit U.R.)

ENCORE-Optional

FIRST CALL

THEATRE OWNER. (*at piano, banging lid*) One Mo' Time. (*He crosses to right of pole with pay checks. THELMA enters first and takes check. She looks displeased. Then MA REED takes check who also looks mad. Then PAPA DU and finally BERTHA, who looks happy. They all sing. Repeat ENCORE VERSE.*)

WARDROBE RUNNING PLOT

DRESSER I   DRESSER II

"BEFORE THE SHOW PRESET"

DRESSER I	DRESSER II
PAPA DU—black face costume: clown white make-up, black face, white gloves, slippers, multi-colored socks, black face tie, kicker pants, white shirt	MA REED—water in dressing room THELMA—cigarettes on prop table ALL CAST—microphones into belts

"BEFORE SHOW BEGINS"

DRESSER I	DRESSER II
BERTHA—gold dress, fur hat, coat, black shoes, gold jewlery. PAPA DU—slacks, vest, shirt, tweed hat	THELMA—pink dress & head band MA REED—black and green fringe dress

"KISS ME SWEET"

DRESSER I	DRESSER II
	THELMA—change to gold dress & headband

"DONT TURN YOUR BACK ON ME"

DRESSER I	DRESSER II
PAPA DU—cake walkin: white slacks, gold shirt, black vest, black jacket, tie, and watch	

SCENE 5 "MAYONNAISE SANDWICH"

DRESSER I	DRESSER II
PAPA DU—take jacket and blackface hat	

"I GOT WHAT IT TAKES"

DRESSER I	DRESSER II
PAPA DU—black face costume	THELMA—purple cape & hat

ONE MO' TIME

> MA REED — sequin dress & head band

DURING "BLACKFACE"

> MA REED — dressing robe

"HE'S FUNNY THAT WAY"

> MA REED — black and green fringe & headband

"DURING "HE'S FUNNY THAT WAY"

BERTHA — kitchen man outfit: white gown, feather fan, white turban, silver shoes, silver jewelry, white gloves

PAPA DU — back into cake walkin outfit with different tie.

BERTHA — kitchen man outfit

"AFTER KITCHEN MAN"

BERTHA — remove kitchen man outfit

DURING "BAND SOLO"

BERTHA — pink dress and headband

THELMA — purple dress and headband

"END OF ACT ONE"

BERTHA — burgundy dress & headband, black shoes and gold jewelry

PAPA DU — blue pin striped suit, white shirt, blue polka dot tie, striped hat

MA REED — black lace dress & headband

"BEFORE THE PARTY"

ALL CAST — party hats, door knock for Thelma

"AFTER PARTY"

MA REED — exotic dance,   MA REED — exotic dance
Two arm snakes, snake head band, finger cymbals, Chinese slippers, top and bottom of costume.

"DURING WHAT IT TAKES TO BRING YOU BACK"

THELMA — white dress & MA REED — black lace headband

"AFTER WHAT IT TAKES"

BERTHA — keyhole gown and robe   BERTHA — keyhole gown and robe
Black slip, robe, silver shoes, silver jewelry, white scarf

"AFTER KEYHOLE"

BERTHA — burgundy dress   BERTHA — burgundy dress

"AFTER PAPA DE DA DA"

MA REED — black robe   BERTHA — red dress with hat, silver shoes and jewelry

STAGE SET REQUIREMENTS

THREE ACTING AREAS (from the actors' prospective, facing audience)
- a) STAGE RIGHT, a five piece band on a platform 7" high
- b) STAGE CENTER, the on stage performing area
- c) STAGE LEFT, the dressing room with a door to on stage and a curtained doorway to off stage dressing area

ENTRANCES
- a) EXTREME STAGE RIGHT, curtained opening leading over the band platform to on stage. For singers entrance.
- b) UP STAGE CENTER, a draped archway leading directly onstage.
- c) UP STAGE LEFT, the dressing room entrance with a door hinged on the on stage side of the casement
- d) EXTREME STAGE LEFT, a doorway with a tattered curtain leading to an off stage dressing area.

BAND AREA CONTAINS:
- a) First row right sits the tuba, center the trumpet, left the clarinet.
- b) Behind right are the drums consisting of base drum, two snare drums, two cymbals on stands and a music stand with light.
- c) Stage left of the drums is the upright piano and adjustable stool. The piano player faces stage left.
- d) There are music stands built into the railing across the front of the band stand for the tuba, trumpet and clarinet. Each music stand has a music light.
- e) Between the trumpet and clarinet is an opening in the railing to allow the either player to enter onstage.
- f) On the right side of the piano sits a tensor light for the piano players use. On top of the piano sits a candelabra.
- g) A microphone is fitted to the clarinet stand and behind the piano for each instrument's amplification.
- h) A rug covers the entire floor.
- i) A monitor speaker sits by the piano facing the drummer.
- j) The right side of the band platform is clear to allow an entrance by a singer.

STAGE CENTER PERFORMANCE AREA:
a) A wooden floor covered with shiny, black linoleum.
b) Small, individual foot lights in reflectors are around the entire stage edge.
c) Extreme up stage center, in front of trumpet player is a 1930 vintage radio microphone on an adjustable stand with enough wire to move down stage center.
d) Extreme up stage center is a column, one foot in diameter from floor to ceiling and covered in mirror cloth. The column is situated between the trumpet and clarinet players.

STAGE LEFT DRESSING ROOM AREA:
a) Two dressing tables 54 inches long, 16 inches deep and 28 inches high made of simple wooden construction. One table faces the audience on the down stage side of the dressing area, the other faces stage right on the right side of the dressing area.
b) Small lights on a cut away frame suggest mirrors on the back of each table.
c) At each dressing table are two chairs with backs and 18 inch high seats.
d) On the stage left wall of the dressing room is built in the third dressing table, 54 inches long, 11½ inches deep and 28 inches high with a mirror.
e) A clothes rack extends at a right angle from the wall on the up stage side of the third dressing table. It is 21 inches long and has a shelf above on which to place a suitcase.
f) Up stage of the clothes rack on the stage left wall of the dressing room is a curtained doorway leading off.
g) Above the third dressing table on the stage left wall is a shelf 67 inches from the floor, 54 inches long and 6½ inches deep.
h) On the up stage wall is a door hinged stage right with knob, stage left. The door opens off stage.
i) Two suitcases sit in the down stage right corner of the area.
j) A waste basket sits under the third dressing table.

PROPS

OFFSTAGE
Working right to left:
- one white stool
- one chrome stool
- one wooden stool w/flask
- one hanger (adjacent to dressing room curtain on railing)

DRESSING ROOM
Closet:
- one Indian shirt
- one ruffled shirt
- one purple cape with fur collar
- one jacket (cake walkin)
- one suitcase w/rope handle containing: one red bow tie, one polka bow tie, one straw hat, one white handkerchief
- one large waste basket

Table #1:
- top shelf—one set of books, one makeup case w/top hat on top, one iron
- bottom shelf-one straw hat, one hat stand w/fur hat, one top hat w/hair, white tails, black tails, one chair w/fur draped over

Table #2:
- one wine bottle w/water
- one cotton towel
- one deck of cards
- two ash trays
- one mirror (gold)
- one box of kitchen matches
- one white beaded bag w/
- one pink headband (Thelma)
- one magazine w/blue comb
- one ladies straw hat
- one green beaded bag w/white gloves
- one hat stand w/purple hat with fur
- one makeup bottle
- one mirror w/brush
- one small waste basket
- one yellow boa over chair

Table #3:
- two suitcases w/purple boa draped over
- one mirror w/headband (Bertha) and white ruffled fan
- one hat stand
- one ash tray
- one mirror on stand
- one mustard headband w/mustard feather
- one plate w/knife
- one jar mayonnaise (small)
- one pint bottle w/coke
- one loaf of bread (small)
- one nail file
- one eyebrow pencil
- one mirror w/brush
- one purple boa over chair

PROPERTY REQUIREMENTS

1) 2 Wooden tables with make-up lights 54" long × 16" deep × 28" high (see design sketch)
2) 18 5 Wooden chairs for dressing room set. Seats to be inches high.
3) Three chairs and one piano stool for band
4) One high stool at 30 inches and 14 inch seat diameter.
5) One low stool 18 inches high with 16 inch seat diameter, of white wicker.
6) 3 Suitcases, the largest no bigger than 21" × 14" × 6"
7) One two light candelabra approximately 10" × 15" high
8) One clap board 6" × 10" (see sketch)
9) One small washboard
10) One adjustable music stand with music light for drummer
11) Three music lights
12) One tensor light for piano
13) One music stand for piano 20" × 12" (see sketch)
14) One 6 foot potted palm
15) One one inch by three inch piece of wood, 12 inches long, to use for door knocker
16) 2 Pitchers with glasses for drinking water, off left and right.
17) One roll of masking tape and one roll of gaffers tape.
18) One small jar of mayonnaise per week (to be refrigerated)
19) One loaf of white bread, sliced per week
20) One waste basket

ONE MO' TIME

SOUND REQUIREMENTS

1) Four wireless microphone systems with transmitters, receivers and small clip on type microphones.
2) Supply of batteries for transmitters as needed.
3) 3 Spare microphones and 3 spare antennas.
4) One 8 channel mixing board with monitor button for each channel, high, middle, and low filters bypass, cue listening button, monitor volume control, attenuation control pot per channel, equalization for each speaker output and monitor output, P.A. microphone at board, and V.U. meters.
5) Intercom system to back stage.
6) Cueing system to spotlight operator and lightboard operator
7) Microphone clipped to clarinet music stand. Meyer dynamic M260.
8) Any brand good piano microphone.
9) Vintage 1930 radio microphone on adjustable stand with fifteen foot of wire.
10) Four or five speaker house amplification system.
11) Two Boise or similar speaker for monitors on stage for performers and one floor mount monitor speaker for band

ON THE TWENTIETH CENTURY
(ALL GROUPS—MUSICAL COMEDY)

Book and Lyrics by ADOLPH GREEN and BETTY COMDEN, Music by CY COLEMAN

17 principal roles, plus singers and extras (doubling possible)—Various sets

Whether performed with elaborate scenery, or on a simple skeletal scale, this brilliantly comic musical can appeal to audiences everywhere. This is truly an extravagant show—but its extravagance lies not in its scenery and physical production, but in the boisterous, tumultuous energy—and in the lush and sprightly energetic surge of its very melodic score. The story concerns the efforts of a flamboyant theatrical impresario to persuade a film star to appear in his next production, to outwit rival producers and creditors, to rid himself of religious nut Letitia Primrose (played by Imogene Coca on Broadway) and Lily's film star boyfriend Bruce Granit (who's as strong in profile as he is weak in brains). And, he must do all this before the famed 20th Century Ltd. reaches NYC! The story, and it's two leading characters—the mad impresario Oscar Jaffe and the love of his life and his greatest star Lily Garland—can be loved and enjoyed by all audiences. "Spectacular . . . funny . . . elegant . . . civilized wit and wild humor."—N.Y. Times. "A perfect musical . . . a gorgeous show!"—N.Y. Post. (#819)

KURT VONNEGUT'S GOD BLESS YOU, MR. ROSEWATER
(MUSICAL SATIRE)

By the creators of LITTLE SHOP OF HORRORS

Book and Lyrics by HOWARD ASHMAN
Music by ALAN MENKEN
Additional lyrics by DENNIS GREEN

10 men, 4 women (principals—also double smaller roles), extras, musicians—Various interiors and exteriors

"One of Vonnegut's most affecting and likeable novels becomes an affecting and likable theatrical experience, with more inventiveness, cockeyed characters, high-muzzle-velocity dialogue and just plain energy that you get from the majority of playwrights."—Newsweek. Eliot Rosewater's a well-intentioned idealist and philanthropic nut—and as president of a multi-million family foundation dispenses money to arcane and artsy-crafty projects. He's also a World War II veteran with a guilt complex, haunted by all this wealth—and also slightly crazy. His outlandish behavior enrages his senator dad, alienates his society-conscious wife—and the money attracts a young, shyster lawyer who tries to divert it to an obscure branch of the family. It portrays Vonnegut's vision of money, avarice and human behavior—as it aims a satirical fusillade at plastic America, fast foods, trademarks, slogans, media blitzes and the follies of materialism. "A charming, delightful, unexpected and thoughtful musical."—N.Y. Post. (#630)

ARTS-HUMANITIES

782.812   Bagneris, Vernel
              One mo' time. Libretto
              One mo' time

R00367 79572

CENTRAL LIBRARY
ATLANTA FULTON PUBLIC LIBRARY